Flickering Flame

Poetic Echoes

DR. K.H. LIM

PARTRIDGE
A Penguin Random House Company

ISBN: Hardcover   978-1-4828-9579-7
           Softcover   978-1-4828-9578-0
           eBook   978-1-4828-9249-9

To order additional copies of this book, contact
Toll Free 800 101 2657 (Singapore)
Toll Free 1 800 81 7340 (Malaysia)
orders.singapore@partridgepublishing.com

www.partridgepublishing.com/singapore

DEDICATION

I dedicate this book to the rock of the family, Song, my royal honey;

Sze Ying, our beloved daughter, and Nai Lee, her devoted husband;

and my three grandchildren Zi Yun, Zi Xun and Jia Jun.

They inspire me to write and to leave a legacy for them to remember.

The love opens from the core,

The nieces, nephews and sibs I adore.

My pen may not yet bless,

My verses need time to express.

PREFACE

Being an avid reader, publishing a book has always been one of my dreams. I did not however, score well in English in school. Perhaps it is for that precise reason that I've felt motivated to pick up where I previously stumbled. In my exploration into the literary world, I have gained much from my love of reading. My enrolment in the Masters Programme has further sharpened my appreciation of literature. The creative space that the Internet has provided has also been pivotal in my development as a writer.

Most of the poems in this collection were written in the past year and they deeply enriched the long and sometimes sterile silences between consultations at the clinic. Most of them are easily understood, drawn as they are, from the common experiences of life. It is my sincere hope that my poetry anthology will inspire some of you to enjoy poetry just as I have.

ACKNOWLEDGEMENTS

I would like to thank Professor Ho Peng Lim, Professor of English at the New INTI Education Group, Malaysia, for reviewing many of my poems. Without his advice and encouragement, the publication of this book may have been further delayed.

I am grateful to Christopher Llyod De Shield, my lecturer (Masters in English) at Open University, Malaysia, and PhD candidate at the Universtiy of Malaya, for reviewing some of my poems and offering much helpful feedback.

My appreciation too to my niece, Adeline Koh Jingyu, for spending a lot of her time painstakingly pointing out many corrections to my poems. Both Jingyu and Chris have encouraged me to move out of the AABB rhyming motif of most of my poems to experiment with free verse.

My appreciation to Madam May Ling Liu, Toronto, Canada, for helping to translate some of my poems into Chinese. We may have hardly known each other, but poetry has brought us together.

CONTENTS

ONE: MUSING

Flickering Flame 1

Dream at Sixty Six 2

Firefly.. 3

Trapped Ego... 4

Who Are We?.. 5

Bucket List 6

Darkness 7

Riddle of Chinese Pictographs 8

Two Faces of Waves 10

Rat and Trap 11

Musing in the Morning 12

Boredom... 13

Fear 14

Loneliness 15

Memory 16

Sober at Sixty Seven.................................... 17

Sermons.. 18

TWO: FAMILY, RELATIONSHIP

Anniversary 19

Love... 20

Love Story 21

An Old Photo 22

Happy Birthday 23

The Ache of Parting 24

Balance 25

Meals: Home or Take-Away 26

Hurt 27

Life and Marriage 28

Intimate Sexuality 29

Hurt Memories 30

THREE: SOCIAL, POLITICAL, MEDICAL

Overcast Sky 33

Registered Trade Mark 34

Old Dad's Rejuvenated Broth 35

Deception 36

The Roads Reaching There 37

"Yes We Can" 38

This Is My Story Of Singapore 40

Unaware 42

Infallible 43

Cuisine and Reflection 45

World's Top 46

Prayers and Faith 47

Prostrating to Prostatism 48

Listen and Silent 49

Fireball. 50

Farewell To A Friend 51

Different World 52

FOUR: CHILDREN

Sharing 53

Lavender, My Love. 54

Crying. 55

Innocence 56

Sisterly Love. 57

Children's Play. 58

Why World of Children 59

FIVE: TRAVEL

Niagara Falls 60

Sunset at Uluwatu, Bali 61

Swiss Border Holiday. 62

Tea Plantation 66

Musing at Mount Kinabalu. 67

Heavenly Tour of Wuyishan. 69

SIX: MY TRANSLATION OF CHINESE CLASSICAL
POEMS AND POEM APPRECIATION

Jiang Jin Jiu (Wine Will Be Served) 70

The Song of Harmony 73

Binging Alone In A Moon-Lit Night 75

Wooing Ospreys. 77

Stopping by Woods on a Snowy Evening: An Appreciation 79

SEVEN: TRANSLATION OF MY POEMS INTO CHINESE
by Madam May Ling Liu

Flickering Flame 82

Firefly. 83

Trapped Ego. 84

Who Are We 85

Bucket List. 86

Riddle of Chinese Pictographs 87

Musing in the Morning 90

Intimate Sexuality 91

Overcast Sky 92

Different World 93

Sharing 94

Sisterly Love. 96

Lavender, My Love. 97

Hurt Memories. 99

Niagara Falls 102

Heavenly Tour of Wuyishan. 103

This Is My Story of Singapore. 104

FLICKERING FLAME

Dance in multiple colours, the flame
flares, blazes and now flickers. Tired light
reflects in life's mirror. An aging nude body,
remorse and horror.
Time to take off working clothes,
in nakedness, freedom flows,
before the embers too weak to kindle
another flame. Soft breeze,
calling, to re-start afresh,
awakens the glow. Soul
crackles and pops, musing
over, the ever-living flame,
the poetry of life.

DREAM AT SIXTY SIX

At sixty six, runs out of
gimmicks, dreams
of colourful lipsticks. Embrace
some discourses. The bosom,
too big and beats
an old horse. Theatrics,
subconscious travel in terrain
beyond the taboos and stereotypes.
The symbols and images, not private,
stigmatise into tattoos, skin
deep, buried in brain circuitry,
since words begin,
hard to peel its colour
off. Other minds,
interpret the dream,
better than the dreamer,
keep dreaming, pout
your lips, for another
colourful life.

FIREFLY

In the shadow

A lone firefly aglow

Transmits coded light

Console a man and his plight.

It's small

The light is not tall.

In darkness:

It beams with brightness

Shining:

In alignment with the divine.

A speck of spark:

Revealing sight for the dark.

Note:

I wrote these verses in response to my friends' queries:

When the heart needs care,
The divine sends an angel there.
O, do not ask, where,
It's everywhere, if aware.

The firefly is just a name,
Nothing is gained in guessing games.
Messages from heart to heart,
This is a one to one art.

TRAPPED EGO

In an uncertain digital age;

Pulled and pushed to the edge.

Forced to shed old skin;

The tattoo is the sin.

Trapped ego fails to glow;

Toss between penumbra and shadow.

Fear to step into the light;

The shadow will be out of sight.

WHO ARE WE?

With our eyes, we see the world not eye to eye;

We hear with our ears, but not listen to the cry.

With our nose, we think more than we smell;

Truth and half-truth are often hard to tell.

Fine cuisine, in delight, we taste;

In haste we eat or end in waste.

We seek what we wish to find;

Divine religion as enshrined.

If lack the art to ask smart;

Your mind is falling apart.

We knock at every door;

Found nothing to adore.

Who are we? Ask again;

Who we are is truly sane.

BUCKET LIST

They insist on looking at my bucket list;

In the hanging coffin is the missing gist.

Live with dignity but die without;

Torment till the last blackout.

Family first, but no time to spare and care;

Relationship is impaired, no love to share.

In living, think you are in control;

In dying, power dissipates into the sinkhole.

Unfulfilled dreams and desire;

Dissonance is hard to rewire.

In living, no urgency for action;

Health, fortune and logic; mere fiction.

Youth and health may not breathe in glamour;

Dreams and hopes are sold by deferral to hanger.

If they still persist on viewing my blacklist;

Ascend and enter my coffin for a tryst.

DARKNESS

The soul trapped in the groove of gramophone;

Deadened sound moans, no music to groan.

Black as record, life full of scratches;

End of the world, all meaning ceases.

No energy to lift up head;

Toss until daybreak in bed.

No laughter, interest slips away;

Dream of Satan watches its prey.

Better dead than suffer;

No anger, but danger.

Hibernate in darkness, shadowy comfort;

The gate keeper lifts up curtain, be alert.

RIDDLE OF CHINESE PICTOGRAPHS

To understand Chinese mind, search

five millennium years of historical find.

Lift the curtains to show the sign,

images and pictures, the hierography,

beginning of civilisation, "wen".

The word, with radicals, in gymnastic

dances, in its own tonal music, flourishes

into art and calligraphy.

Synchronisation, symbols and semantics

tango in pair or group in trio.

Pictogram evolves into logogram

and ideogram,

the birth of an ancient language,

a proud civilisation.

The Yin and Yang culture,

stresses and distresses in harmony, reflected in "wen".

The word, to "eat",

formed by twin radicals,

meaning to beg a mouthful,

reflects a continuing history

of poverty,

changing dynasties, internal wars,

foreign plunder, rape:

the Chinese learn through harsh experience.

To keep citizens civil,

leaders provide grains to meet their needs.

The importance of food,

feast and cuisine culture stays within the family,

and kins. Again,

the ideogram for destiny, describes

the person's first priority: To

bow to what fate inscribes, or listen to

oral commandments from above. Fatalism

is not Chinese philosophy: When impoverished,

change, rise in mutiny, be disobedient; In disorder,

risks beget opportunities, to transform

fate and open freedom's gate. Yet

human beings have limitations.

Things we may be unable

to change. Destiny is final acceptance

when all efforts fail.

Language and culture, nourish one another.

The ancient pictograph, eyes into Chinese mind.

吃　食　命

chī　　shí　　ming

eat　　food　　destiny

TWO FACES OF WAVES

Waves rides on waves towards the shore;

Surge and spume at the beach, roll and roar.

Or, in angry display of its awesome might;

Ascend high to sky, the earth splits in fright.

Divine punishment, toxic debris flow and drift;

Connect by sin, the wrath warns moral uplift.

Wise use of energy, lifestyle divine or vile;

The sea regains its pristine beauty with smile.

To navigate in sea or land, guided by beacon;

Do not let the bastions become your prison.

RAT AND TRAP

A ranky rat is caught in a mesh trap;
Fat cats have lost the skill to snap.

The creature terrorist is put to rest;
Strange that Noah's Ark allows pests.

All beings are created equal;
That includes damsels and evil.

Heirs to kamma, all are related;
Fortune may turn for the wretched.

If not kill and let pests go;
The neighbours' faces furrow.

Or return and damage more;
Kindness, not adored, but sore.

Pricked conscience of moral teaching;
Stress the good, not uniting but dividing.

MUSING IN THE MORNING

Queue up at a Singapore food stall;
My joints crack by the slow crawl.
Here, the porridge-dish is the best;
Juicy meatballs salivate down the chest.
A cup of kopi-o to uplift the morning spirit;
Day's merit is sustained by good habits.
Flip through the pages for home news;
View rapes, robberies and racial abuse.
Unable to find a page worthy of reading;
The trash hurts the eyes and unnerving.
Tears that braggarts fill the cabinets;
Discard and wrap them with blankets.

BOREDOM

Repeat same routine in the office;

same predictability in same premise,

the soul is dead in timeless infinity,

doses of stimuli to escape from ennui.

The self is angry with stale stillness;

lethargic body in dreamless sleepiness.

Savoury gossips to serve as good starter;

exercises, coffee, wine and sex, no better.

Odysseus whined at Calypso's seduction,

promise of paradise, a disguised prison.

Mind hungers for changes and varieties;

demons unhappy, demand different fairies.

Malaise is dissatisfaction in the moment;

time flows, the moment is but a figment.

FEAR

Severe pain woke him,
the vomits splashed,
over the bowl and floor,
never happened before.
Self-assured when settled
fast, no fuss until it recurred
thrice in a month, the fear of
medical prison in post pension.
Family record was malignant,
lost weight and waist, until
the pants dropped. Had lived life
to the full, and would be a fool, if
lack guts to scope and scan the
body. The culprit was not the
feared, unspeakable big "C". The scan
showed foie gras, rest considered
normal. It was strange role reversal,
the bacteria ate, without causing
deep puncture holes in stomach.
Felt fast relieved, without his usual
letting go. Without fear to moderate,
the urgency of change, the lifestyles,
the placing of priorities, the second
chance of living were mere passing
moments, until tidal wave arrived.

LONELINESS

Landscape seen through a glass window;
the wide social network flows, illuminating
homographic crowd in shows. Interactions,
hobbies and interests take sides, heads bog
down in over sensitive situations, ego factors
fall out of belonging, find unfulfillment, build
isolated islands. Even hermits change their
attitudes meditating in solitude, meaningless to
live in molehill mountains. Six billion bulbs,
fancy can't find a few that glows and warms
one's heart. The slow nagging down feel, cries
out for that strange fairness, but, seeps deeper into
the marrow, and the soul suffers a caffeine-like
withdrawal. Stay engaged to get back the kick,
even if support is harder to come by with the
impending and uncertain changing of clothes.

MEMORY

Takes hours to find non missing glass;

He confuses the time and date of class.

The slips get more and more often;

Annoyed when point out in the open.

Garrulously, he talks about the past;

Sure, he narrates ancient history fast.

An eerie sky in evening with lost grandeur.

A shimmering Libra will soon be obscured.

Tip of the tongue, but cannot retrieve;

Feeling deceived by memory thieves.

Blackout causes the mind to jitter;

The pillow partner, he can't remember;

Shadows and words become blur.

Confusion and fear cause anger.

Return to childhood with wet nurse;

Not knowing ghost in mirror is a curse.

SOBER AT SIXTY SEVEN

Alive and thrive at sixty seven,

Not void of reason and passion.

Dream about peace in the country;

Big mouths abound, dine is not easy.

The melting pot has cracked;

The salad bowl is the next act.

Vinegar and virgin oil to dress;

Arguments augment the stress.

Balsamic is not fermented wine;

Partake fine dine, don't whine.

Stay sober to share dreams together;

Glamorise pickiness, the course, no better.

SERMONS

In an unseen dais,

sermons vibrate across

square, testifying

unbiased truth,

raining from above,

the decoders reign

supreme, in sensurround,

the fervour of faith,

chosen favour and flavour

pacify the burdened soul,

in everlasting bliss.

Protect your kingdom,

sing in unison your anthem,

violence against the other.

Voices attuned to the amplitude,

harmonises background music,

changed attitude for benefit.

ANNIVERSARY

Hand-in-hand, we walk our age in grace;

Eyes and ears compliment each embrace.

Thirty-seven years, mother in you, toil and pamper;

Honing culinary and sewing skill, all cares prosper.

Man, at a fragile age, wishes to be cajoled;

As much as tender souls hope to be consoled.

Chopsticks, the dancing duo, are cherished as a pair;

New or wear, they move and share for mutual welfare.

Note:

A pair of chopsticks connotes the "yin" (feminity) and "yang" (masculinity), but also implies passivity and activity in complementary ways to complete an act.

LOVE

A three-generation family gathers near the sea;

Relate in Michelin, sip spicy wine and tannic tea.

Finds fulfillment? Happy ending in fairy land;

Contentment brews intoxication in sunken sand.

To our dear ones, meet eye to eye, share;

Sisyphus labours his boulder, no hands to spare.

An explorative journey, the post not mark;

Return to Adam's Garden, the burden ego park.

In Maslow's elevator, passing phases in ways strange.

Love, rooted in gravity, may rotate but never change.

LOVE STORY

An album of poetic photos is sent by post;

"The Story of Love" is treasured utmost.

Turning the pages down memory lane;

An elegant pendant shines again and again.

The jewel, heir to our cherished care;

Her career and attributes show some flair.

The nuptials bless her with an initial charming pair;

Lineage begets another heir for families to share.

From roots to fruits she showers her love;

In fertile soil with rain and shine from above.

AN OLD PHOTO

My lady stands behind me, her hands on my shoulder;

I sit in front of her, protecting her against all weather.

The snow-capped Rockies reflect our silvery hair;

The serenity of the lake captures the pair with care.

An old photo flashes reminiscences;

It's silly not to treasure one another's presence.

We all wish to recapture our lost moment;

Do not let the fragrance of love lie dormant.

HAPPY BIRTHDAY

Gifts of love to grace your day;

Universal family values to stay.

All your aspiration turns roses;

Sing love melodies in praises.

O, you are truly the family pillar;

Nurse and care without whimper;

Go and seek your dream;

Fulfil your wishes and esteem.

Unfold your pristine wings;

Above sixty, sparks and swings.

Note:

This birthday poem begins with the initial alphabets of the person's name in each line.

THE ACHE OF PARTING

Pervading fragrance of water jasmine, the home-again feeling religiously inspires;

White snowy petals blossom among the rejuvenated greens in garden many aspire.

Fronds from red and yellow palms dance and sing with the wind in unison;

Birds attune the chirping, butterflies flap and squirrels have fun in the sun.

The old carved wooden door greets the return with grin.

Enters the home where love and friendship begin.

Green foliage hangs and flies from high;

Koi swim in pond-water from the sky.

The harmony of cascading water splashes and flashes many memories;

The hall of mirrors reflects the weekend gathering here with glories.

The oaky serpentine winds up the majestic stairs;

The mansion maintenance wears out lone old pairs.

Three decades, we have parked our hearts;

It is a dream house and hard to part.

BALANCE

Work rides opposite of family in seesaw;

Balance one against the other is flaw.

The ups and downs, a natural pair;

Yin and Yang embrace in air.

Quality, quantity hard to measure in time;

Only mad mathematicians find it fine.

Money and responsibility are sheer pressure;

Work shakes hands with leisure, a treasure.

Dr. Jekyll and Mr. Hyde are hidden selves;

The motivations, surface each out of shelves.

The fad of balanced life is good concoction;

A mixologist knows neat or cocktail potions.

MEALS: HOME OR TAKE-AWAY

Global musing on why men keep mistresses;

The word misses or hides a million stresses.

Before the grave, give life a memorable crave.

Fearing death and lost opportunity, act brave.

Fagged by chores, the nagging soars;

Build walls, open old and new sores.

To satiate unfulfilled kisses;

Glutamate soups to hit the dishes.

Gastronomic novelty to improve taste;

Pleasure is thirst, non-chaste ends in waste.

Home cuisine less decorative and spicy;

The recipe quenches thirst to stay healthy.

HURT

I am hurt

Because I care

Your indifference is my despair.

I am hurt

Because my needs are not met

Yet you think I am mad.

I am hurt

Because my efforts end in pain

Yet you insist I reap gain.

I am hurt

Because I suffer frustration

You lack proper reciprocation.

You build your wall and you quip

Unaware that relationship has slipped.

Now, we face the end of living

It's late to regret the sad beginning.

LIFE AND MARRIAGE

Falling in love is blind;

The pimples appear divine.

The wet towels thrown on the floor;

Butts, empty cans provoke eyesore.

Replays the drama of the hurt;

Bruises, habits, insults and dirt.

Erects high walls to forgive the person;

Foul mouth recites and repeats in action.

Marriage roller coaster may be rife;

Medication replaces the quest for life.

When the relate and sadism turn sour;

We cling to the fort in the last hour.

Family is the first and last contact;

To comfort us in the final ugly attack.

Next in line are relatives and friends;

And the communities we depend and defend.

To relate well is thus to live well;

Simplicity does not sound the bell.

INTIMATE SEXUALITY

In the middle of the night,

the spirit, awakened by the heat,

seizes the moment,

with tender might. Inflamed,

fullness feeling, the spinal

flame engorged. Heavy breathing,

bed dishevelled with pillow mate,

touches and teases, opens

her heart, embedded, art flows

and glows, gifting exudates. Bathed

in harmonious bliss,

murmuring their kisses.

HURT MEMORIES

Chaotic hurt memories

run through

her mind, her heart

like a reel of endless movie,

in selective, seductive replay.

She clings to the hurt,

the unwanted pain,

like a bruised, bored cat

plays with a frightened rat.

The act of compulsive

remembering

hurt feelings, betrayal for

love and hate is

so convoluted,

so enduring,

the chest pain

nagging incessantly,

like bloated air

gargling in the gut.

Unable to forget

past hurt,

continues to register

the same blame,

and blaming game,

again and again,

like melted ice, thawed and

refrozen with each chill.

Overrides love feelings

in the past, present or

future, the freedom of what

to remember, to forget

what must or need to be

forgotten, or unremembered.

To run or step down

on a hate treadmill, for the

hearts and pulses,

do relate or resonate

in tortuous circuitries

not easy to control,

smart tricks turn smarting.

A simple apology,

a sincere remorse,

a big step backwards,

without many words

or thoughts. It's so easy

and yet very, very hard

to make that move

to let go

of hurt, and

to hold on

to the healing power

of love, forever

so bitter sweet.

OVERCAST SKY

The ink stains with an indelible memory;

Clean election for change is washable folly.

The pointing fingers cast their votes;

Only banknotes can capsize the boats.

Flying aliens steal the show;

The tsunami fails to overthrow.

Game is never fair, but troops spared;

Power does blare, a desperate dare.

No drumming gong or banging cymbal;

Corruption, not colour, is the battle bugle.

REGISTERED TRADE MARK

Birth rights, cast in stone,

made in heaven, one and

only one trade mark. Magic

password, exclusive, to open

the gates of power,

the might and dominance,

from the barrel. Grand masters

gerrymander the talk, lame ducks,

take turns, to waddle in cat walks;

Bagged bullion, from the coffers,

as hand-outs or bail outs,

from brethren to cronies;

Disgruntled boarders, stay easy,

air out or get out.

OLD DAD'S REJUVENATED BROTH

The curry sits cold in the old coloured melting pot;

Sauté with spices and chilies, the recipe is spicy hot.

The cooks and cronies relish their fantastic feast;

Devouring God-given meat, mouths stained with grease.

Leaving their kind hungry, with gravies to eat;

The elite care only for the power and the seat.

Incite and blame to snatch the others' cake;

Shouting slogans, lazy to learn to bake.

Voices echoing in strange racial octane;

Confusing issues between the brain and drain.

The table tumbles and the pie crumbles;

The people finally realise the true fumblers.

The new chef, with rejuvenated broth, proclaims:

The one-for-all recipes win some claim.

But the culinary is poor and the broth stale;

Crocodile's tears mixed with foxtails and fail.

Kitchen and cabinet fumes with odours;

The room remains stale when the cooking's over.

DECEPTION

She reveals the white and red;

The aroma from the shake spreads.

Her full bodied is sensuous to break;

The mouthful is gulped down in an intake.

A royal salute is coaxed to touchdown.

The burden is lifted, light but not drown.

Feel afloat in a flying mythical bird;

Dream about what is not absurd.

Can hardly count in the moment;

Any place where corruption not rampant.

Disorientated in my place of birth;

Some wrong blue cards have lesser worth.

Educated with an open mind and passion;

For half century, rights to match the sermon.

You are drunk because you bear the grievances in silence.

Cry out aloud in unison to show the power of your presence.

THE ROADS REACHING THERE

Brown, yellow and black of both gender;

March the right road with such wonder.

The gases fired shed their shared tears;

Cry for a crumbling structure without fear.

The cannons they dare to defy;

The myth of racial divide to rectify.

At the Square, hundreds of hearts gather;

To confront a corrupt power together.

And, though, I am not there;

I take another path to meet somewhere.

"YES WE CAN"

Yes, we can

To stay supreme

We can act extreme.

Terrorists, we fight

Justify our means and might.

Spy drones bomb any territory

Burn to Stone Age in any boundary.

Whether suspect or innocent

Trust on intelligent judgement.

Yes, we can

To stay supreme

We are free to be extreme.

We spy on our enemies

Real or imaginary, the Chinese

And the North Koreans alike

Whoever and whatever we dislike.

Create stories and war games

We inflame and blame.

Hell to these manipulators, cheaters

Yellow horde Cyber attackers.

Yes, we can

To stay supreme

Nothing is extreme.

We watch even our allies

Any citizen who defies.

First amendment is history

Bright legacy becomes phony.

Yes, we can

To stay at the top

No one can stop.

God bless the good American.

THIS IS MY STORY OF SINGAPORE

Died in the sands of Singapore

Melquiades left his parchment,

the alchemy, deep in the swamps,

for the wise and diligent

to discover, magic and wisdom,

the rebirth of another

city state. The ancient prince,

by the power of a company clerk,

transformed the cat he saw

into a lion, and named it so,

and hocus pocus,

the tears of the mentor,

yellow petals and gold fishes,

into a merlion. Accepted

hard working coolies and rejects,

from coastal China, the brains

from the north and nearby land,

without discrimination of colour,

turning the barren into a

modern metropolis, a tiny

dotty island, called united

constituencies, lasting

almost half a century.

It will endure, as long as

aware of genealogical

incest and corruptions,

of small varied population,

able to internally tuned,

externally rewired in an

ever changing world.

UNAWARE

Unaware

The pen touched a nerve

The reaction was over severe.

Unaware

It was a Party talk

The joy overstepped someone's walk.

Unaware

Knowledge hot on the lips

Art of relate cold on finger tips.

Unaware, unaware

But how to beware

Colour of others' hidden wear.

INFALLIBLE

I am infallible.

Don't tempt me

to fall

into the hole,

the sin,

polluted sinkholes.

My life is

spotless,

white sheet in snow,

pure pious prostration.

I am holy,

not without holes,

build barriers,

chant and follow

precepts and concepts.

Don't lure me to

the temptations,

the spirit is strong,

but the body weak.

My spirituality,

whitewashed,

bleached, secretive,

born again,

so untouchable,

until you show me,

hell, the fire of

life.

CUISINE AND REFLECTION

Frozen behind the harmonious subtlety is the subterfuge;

The raw bloody freshness compels the ocean to seek refuge.

The culinary art balances the gastronomic delight;

The guiltless politeness and supremacy eclipse the light.

Absolute unquestioned loyalty causes the fall;

Grey hairs and right wingers rule the fireball.

The elegance and technology earn worldwide respect;

Without soul searching the stains are too proud to defect.

WORLD'S TOP

Surrounded by

man-eating sharks,

white angelic jellyfishes and anemones,

psychedelic coloured sea creatures and divers,

my granddaughters were amazed

we remained dry and safe. No leak in the system,

absolutely not allowed. This tiny spot boasted

many of the world's top, feared

of being dropped or flopped,

in the rat maze of technologies,

where culture was uprooted, and

human touch submerged in oceanic floor,

shipwrecked and formed fossilised reef corals.

For

the Empire must not sink.

Corruption and "chope" brought society to the brink,

Even my grandson's spontaneous smile,

Would show the human world not an aquarium,

where feelings, relations and idiosyncrasies

could be so easily managed, protected and controlled

like fishes in experimental marine museum.

The largest window opened from hearts,

that were free right from the start.

PRAYERS AND FAITH

Fragrant incenses ascend;

Faith burns from head to end.

Pious supplication fills the air;

Offering and request trade in pair.

Fly with congenial change;

Rust and rot do derange.

True to self but prime to body;

Crippled crossing Mount Meru boldly.

In uncertainties, strange not to pray;

Ask and knock when love moves away.

PROSTRATING TO PROSTATISM

Life begins with terminal drips;

Redefined by making frequent trips.

To learn from principle: "First thing first";

The priority is not about hunger or thirst.

It's exploring the nearest proper place;

Rushing may wet the pants and face.

Blush not if you really suffer a flush;

Pamper your life before the crush.

There are things that enlarge; things that shrink;

When bodies are out of sync, the flow either kinks or stinks.

We adjust and learn to accept changes with grace;

With help, dance all our way into the comforter's embrace.

LISTEN AND SILENT

Listen: the first step in learning;

The secret is in word reversing.

Aware: responses and reactions;

Care in choice of options.

Replies we like and loathe;

Smart to learn from both.

Need both facts and tact;

Humility will make impact.

Note: Some cautionary words to junior doctors.

FIREBALL

Her tender scalp sore and hurt;

The craters raw, pus spurts.

The wound spins a small fireball;

Render the hair and hearts to fall.

Wound worsens, lumps swollen;

The lotion and solution are in question.

Attuned to her pain, pray for recovery;

Healing words will help soothe her worry.

FAREWELL TO A FRIEND

Not long ago we whined and dined together;

You were quiet but still full of laughter.

The sudden news that you left the class;

Hastening to meet mates on heavenly pass.

When you were assemblyman, too busy for all;

The brawl in politics forced you to the wall.

In public office, you had no private life;

The wildlife and nightlife was rife.

The stroke jolted your balance;

Fame repaid in hidden grievance.

The mask you wore not without cost;

The lost self turned into exhaust.

We may be transiently apart;

Farewell, you are alive in our hearts.

DIFFERENT WORLD

Allured by the azure bright;

Emitted from distant tunnel light.

Mother, in her best, stands there;

Legendary friends meet with flair.

Serene and light, float in mid-air;

Tearing teens weep vigil over body;

The wind caresses their hair in lobby.

The seeping energy forbids long stay;

To another world, the breeze flies away.

SHARING

Do not hold my hand
Don't bite
Only a gentle lick

The lips touch
The soft sweet feel
Hard to resist
A steal
Melt inside the mouth
Joy in the hearts

She pulls away
Keep promises

But how—
To persuade
A charming reluctant child
To share
Her favourite chocolate cone

Relishing and dripping
Down on her cold hand
With her loving and salivating
Grandpa

LAVENDER, MY LOVE

She withdraws
to her quiet own corner,
stands tip-toed,
head bowed low,
sulking in silence,
mumbling her own
grievances, for a while.
She cries out aloud,
for their love,
and sole attention.
Hug me,
cuddle me,
carry me,
Only me, first.
She shies away from people,
no longer enjoys
school, steals time away
from home,
deprives the child,
more joy to play
in sweet, safe comfort,
for love has to be
shamelessly shared,
with the birth of
baby brother.

CRYING

Hug and snug, my baby, do not cry;

Colic? Hunger? And the nappy is dry.

Cry not, my baby, let mom feed;

Cry not baby, let us sleep.

All cause pried, and tirelessly tried.

INNOCENCE

It's bliss to watch how little children meet;

Wherever they are, they just play and greet.

They are so spontaneous and so trusting;

Their innocence is indeed amazing.

They have no barrier about race;

In any country they go, or in any place.

Their thoughts are clear and without fear;

Their sincere hearts are dear and we cheer.

SISTERLY LOVE

The breeze hums outside the windows;

Fronds play ghosts with their shadows.

Lightning and thunder pound their might;

Pray the gods target the right site.

How my darlings spend their restive fortnight;

With no scooter ride at home confined to excite.

Puzzle how the bad witch infects her mouth;

Blisters and craters, pain to partake and shout.

Lock herself in room, the baby sister is well;

For a six year-old, her love really rings the bell.

Toddler sends messages from balcony to shutter.

Wishing her sister well and out on scooter together.

Note:

Recently, my elder granddaughter suffered from Hand, Foot and Mouth disease,
and was barred from attending her kindergarten. Her toddler sister was also
prevented from attending her pre-kinder school as preventive health. In her own
quarantine in her room, they both miss one another much.

CHILDREN'S PLAY

My sweetie will visit us this week;

We play pretend, hide and seek.

Imposes own rules, follow like a class of sheep;

Play the game she fancies, or she will weep.

Her self-centredness slowly sways away;

And can be critical of other's way.

Through play, she learns to trust and share;

Segregate them, their worlds lack fun fare.

WHY WORLD OF CHILDREN

She continues to ask why, and why;

Her inquisitive mind is never shy.

Not bullet proof by salvoes of bombard;

Many mothers will fall flat on the yard.

Why do we love another more, or hate the other;

The adult world differs and often hard to ponder.

From her story books, simple replies are sufficient;

The talk-time helps, not answers that are brilliant.

Why do adults often in battle?

To her, the world is simple.

She plays, invites and accepts;

Not knowing precepts and concepts.

Welcome to the why, why, why game;

World of innocence cannot remain same.

NIAGARA FALLS

At the Horseshoe

voluminous, voluptuous downpour

worshippers from all over congregate to adore

the raging rapids, the thunderous torrent,

beats her drum. The smoky mist stirs up her charm.

The water glitters, splashes

her luster, her pristine beauty,

prides across the continents.

Dare to crash

her bottom, by boat.

Or walk at the edge of the Fall,

risk just to get near, feel the thrill,

of life. The seduction thaws

the ice of mundane,

The wild has power,

brings hot blood in cold routine.

SUNSET AT ULUWATU, BALI

Stripped and stretched on the hill top turf;

Old bones attuned to the sound of raging surf.

Peer at the heavens, face to face;

The world, downside up, seems a strange place.

The sun glows, like a golden glimmering ball;

Gradually cool and losing its heat and gall.

It dives into the ocean unaware;

Suddenly, vanishing into nowhere.

In my sunset years with sealed fate;

Will I pass through the needle into heavenly gate?

Will I rise again from the mountain?

Like Lazarus arising behind the tomb curtain.

Lost in reverie, darkness soon swallows this great earth;

In this land of eerie beauty and mirth, terrorists find a berth.

SWISS BORDER HOLIDAY

Landed in Zurich in the morning rain;

Pulled our luggage to the next train.

Fog could hardly hide the pretty lakes and hills;

Passing images were serene but our hearts not still.

The eyes ("I") snapped every moving scenes;

The outside turned insight for what's seen.

The digital was easier to delete and retrieve;

Hard to compete with the modern, yet full of thrive.

Arrived in Luzern around noon;

In the drizzle found the nearby hotel soon.

Walked reflexology in cobbled lanes;

Ancient painting on shop fronts and window panes.

Well fed fairy swans and ducks paddled in the cold lake;

Shoppers delighted in designers and bought what money could take.

Travelled via buses and Euro-rail to Oberland;

Zigzagged three days in this fairy Swiss land.

Glacier falls, carved snow animals, to reach Europe's peak;

Lived between clouds, heaven and earth, to hear God speak.

Spoke without tongue, here and there, for each to seek;

The nameless experience not meant for the meek.

At Interlaken, we took a pleasant boat ride;

Watches, chocolates, wood carving, fondue were Swiss pride.

In Berne, Goethe cathedral, tower clocks and bear park;

Enjoyed and returned to Oberland often in the dark.

The water cascaded and reflected its white silvery fall;

Dark ink calligraphy hanged from hill tops was tall.

Even lovers had to separate and depart;

Life moved on whether easy or hard;

Moving on we rented a small car:

Fancy how we squeezed in would win star.

To Beaune, we drove four hours to the French border;

GPS, the modern god, guided the way further.

In 1443, the impressive Hospice turned museum was built for the poor;

The wards, pharmacy, halls, kitchen, prayer rooms took hours to tour.

At Cheval Noir, we dined until late in the night;

With Pinot Noir, we found the way to guest house right.

Birthday lunch at Lameloise was gustatory and culinary par excellence;

Such rare indulgence with the family was balance and life fragrance.

Six amuse bouche paired with six appetizers to whet salivation;

Foie gras hugged with sweet bread, shoot and figs, in culinary fashion.

Cod bathed in coconut oil, swam with cuttlefish in the soup;

Tender lamb, tarnished with plants, apples, red onions sauntered with whoop.

Fine burgundy cheese with avant desserts of ten finger-licking kinds;

Parted this proud traditional Michelin with nostalgia entwined.

At St. Remy and Les Baux, we had a romantic visiting day;

Visiting villages, palace, Abbeys and the hospital where Van Gough stayed.

The mystery sunk-hole at Fontaine was a pleasant attraction;

Partaking pastries, smoked meat, in morning market was good distraction.

Ancient Roman theatres, castle ruins, viaducts, degustation menus for taste;

Vineyards and cellars, vintage white and red, won our praise.

Travelled south to coastal Nice, near the Mediterranean Sea;

Palm tree lined promenade, pebble beach, palaces, the rain not foresee.

Spectacular architectures, statutes, with vagabonds slept in cold enclaves.

Despite opulence, did not set foot on Monaco: place where F1 and gamblers crave.

Tunnels after tunnels, on elevated highways, town houses perched on terraced hills;

Crossed Como, Italy, GPS lost reception, but I pad found way to hotel without frills.

A hurried breakfast, rushed to the double deck ferry touring the picturesque lake;

Again villas and mansions perched on waterfronts and nice pictures to show and take.

At Bellagio, a rich hamlet, licking a creamy cone with a reluctant child in fun sharing;

Half day wasted in fixing a damaged fuse, but compensated by factory outlet shopping;

Reached Swiss city, Lugano, the ladies fazed by the cold breeze, preferred to shop;

Contemplated "life" sculpture: fusion of symbols meaning hard to tell bottom from top.

Drove through tunnels, serpentine roads, returned to Zurich before late;

Enjoyed the old city and its past grandeur, appeared well than the new by any rate.

Kunsthaus Art Gallery, old and new masters showed their creativity with grace and skill;

Impressionism, surrealism, abstractions, cubism: more imagination, flair and thrill.

Shops closed on Sundays, the airport was a destination for dine and last hour purchases;

Farewell to a happy sojourn across three nations, our driver cum planner won praises.

Note:

We travelled to Zurich. At Interlaken (Switzerland), we hired a sedan, but didn't know it was so small. We managed to squeeze all our travel belongings in, plus 5 adults and 1 child, and toured around Switzerland, border towns of France and Italy (2400 kms). The long poem was a record of our epic journey.

TEA PLANTATION

Strolls along the slippery, serpentine trail;
Rows and rows of tea shrubs pruned to scale.
Hills descend on valleys, valleys ascend on hills.
Miles and miles of verdant wonder: fill with thrill.
Morning sun crimsons the yonder horizon;
Landscape brightens, but bleak with fiction.
From a peak, easier to watch another summit;
Stands at a height, humble enough to see limit.
Descends down the valley to continue the walk;
Nature and nurture deliver their silent talk.

MUSING AT MOUNT KINABALU

The mist

In its appearing and disappearing phantasm

Veiling and unveiling its bridal sanctum

The summit

A pair of lovers' head

Embedded in one another's stead

The climbers

Lured to take refuge

In a majesty, healing mundane deluge

The tourist

Postured for snapshots

With furious camera onslaughts

The narrator

Standing, at the foothills, ponders

Wandering the search for meaning, wonder!

The omnipresent comparison

Top, mid, bottom and below

Doing, undoing, not doing, fast or slow

The restless mind

Jigsaw interpretations of own belief

Holding the almighty for true or false relief

As human non-beings

Reality and delusion

Escaping all from Eden's Garden

Yet—

In this world,

Powerful personalities exert their influence

Their misjudgment leaving grievances

The Law

Of nature, religion, politics and the knighted

Forgetting the lessons of the blessed

The mist

HEAVENLY TOUR OF WUYISHAN

Sonorous through crevices and caves, the missing tiger's roars;

We mount, without any martial arts, up the heavenly tour [i].

Peep at narrow light aperture, no goddess taking bath.

The bodhisattva at the peak forbids our ascending path.

At the foothills, arhat [ii] tea and rocky fungus, are on promote;

Six bushes of imperial red robes [iii] on cliff are cutthroat.

A six-seater bamboo raft rows down from upstream;

Gorgeous gorges, turn and twist, meander in daydreams.

Calligraphy competes with misty rocky formation in bliss;

The hanging coffin [iv] reminds earthly souls what is amiss.

Note:

[i] Wuyi, the name of the mountain, is homophonic with martial arts. Mount Wuyi is situated in the Fujian Province of South China. It is one of the 43 UNESCO heritage sites in China, out of a total of more than 962 in the world. The mountain path to the peak is named as "Heavenly Path" due to its height. The river in the valley has nine turns and eighteen twists, with natural and man-made sceneries, such as calligraphy. The hanging coffin, at the end of the ride, is a powerful image and metaphor. When the wind passes through the caves, the sound produced is similar to the roaring of a tiger.

[ii] "Tie Lou Han" (Iron Arahant) is a type of fermented red tea. Arahants are also enlightened beings according to Buddhism.

[iii] Fermented dark red oolong tea are high grade tea meant for emperors only (now for leaders).

[iv] These coffins are cantilevered out of plucked wooden planks and are partially hidden inside rock enclaves. They are 3750 years old.

JIANG JIN JIU (WINE WILL BE SERVED)

Poem by Li Bai (Tang Dynasty—701-762 AD)

Have you not seen?

The downpour into the Yellow River, a heavenly scene

Its torrent gushes into the ocean

And the return stream not reckon

(Have you not seen?)

The weariness in your parents' white lock

Their aging is a sad sight in shock.

At the dawn of life, as black as silk, shines

At dusk, shows snowy lines.

When happy opportunities appear

Fulfill them here and dear

Do not let our golden cups emptied of wine

When face under such bright moonshine.

The talent I am blissfully endowed

My skill will facilitate what I have avowed

A thousand taels of gold may be squandered

Its value, in kinds and ways, will be recovered

Gastronomical delight of beef and lamb is served

A binge of three hundred cups will be observed.

To Master Cen,

To Scholar Dangiu

Wine is now served

Do not be reserved

I shall sing to both soon

Attentively, your ears, attune

Palatial music, fine cuisine, is not grand

Wish we are forever drunk and in dreamland

In ancient times, lonely sages are not remembered.

Only wine drinkers have their names sculptured.

In the past, Prince Chen held a grand banquet in his palace

In pursuit of hedonistic indulgence par excellence

At a cost of ten thousand silver pieces

For a mere dipperful of wine dashes

As your host, money is never in doubt

To procure more wine for our bout.

My spotted horse and fur worth a thousand

My son to trade and buy wine on errand

Together we shall drown away

Share the million miseries of bygone days.

李白：将进酒

君不見， 黃河之水天上來，

奔流到海不復回？

君不見， 高堂明鏡悲白髮，

朝如青絲暮成雪？ 人生得意須盡歡，

莫使金樽空對月， 天生我材必有用，

千金散盡還復來。

烹羊宰牛且為樂， 會須一飲三百杯。

岑夫子！ 丹丘生！

將進酒； 君莫停。

與君歌一曲， 請君為我側耳聽。

鐘鼓饌玉不足貴， 但願長醉不願醒。

古來聖賢皆寂寞， 惟有飲者留其名。

陳王昔時宴平樂， 斗酒十千恣讙謔。

主人何為言少錢？ 徑須沽取對君酌。

五花馬， 千金裘。

呼兒將出換美酒， 與爾同消萬古愁。

Note:

Jun is translated as "you", more gender neutral, instead of "gentleman". I hope my translation makes recitation in English smoother.

THE SONG OF HARMONY (Shui Diao Ge Tou)

Poem by Su Dong Po (Song Dynasty—1037-1101 AD)

Whence the next luminous moon appeared?

Raising my wine-cup, to the blue sky, I cheered.

I knew neither the gate of heavenly abode,

Nor how the evening in celestial years, decode.

I desired to surf on the wind in my blissful return;

The exquisite jade and jasper might damage was my concern.

The high altitude with its cold was my deterrence;

Dancing in its shadows, the transcendence in transience.

The lights revolved around its amber pavilion;

Through its low lattices, it scattered in zillion.

Its reflection flickered on my sleepiness;

The fulfillment and separation were blameless.

Happiness and depression, union and separation, are human
restlessness;

The imperfect moon displayed its changing brilliance and
infrequent roundness.

Such imperfection was revealed since bygone years;

We only cherished to live longer and what we endeared.

To share the bond such brilliance brought;

Despite living miles apart, perfection forever sought.

明月几时有，把酒问青天。

不知天上宫阙，今夕是何年。

我欲乘风归去，又恐琼楼玉宇，

高处不胜寒，起舞弄清影，何似在人间。

转朱阁，低绮户，照无眠。

不应有恨，何事长向别时圆。

人有悲欢离合，月有阴晴圆缺，此事古难全。

BINGING ALONE IN A MOON-LIT NIGHT

Tang poem by Li Bai

Among the flowers, there's a pot of wine.

I binge alone: in absence of friends and relate.

Raising my cup, propose a toast to the moon.

Its image and my shadow complete a trinity.

They are oblivious to my drunken pleasure.

The shadows tango with the body.

We are transient partners.

We seek instant gratification.

Whenever I sing, the moon stays motionless.

Whenever I dance, the shadows tumble on one another.

In regaining awareness, the trio commutes delight.

They part company only when intoxicated.

We hope to foster eternal bonds.

And seek unforgettable communion in timeless galaxies.

花間一壺酒
獨酌無相親
舉杯邀明月
對影成三人
月既不解飲
影徒隨我身
暫伴月將影
行樂需及春
我歌月徘徊
我舞影零亂
醒時同交歡
醉後各分散
永結無情遊
相期邈雲漢

Note:

History narrated that the poet died from drowning in one of his binges.

WOOING OSPREYS

SHI JING (Book of Poems): (Zhou Dynasty: 1122-256 BC)

"Guan, guan", the Ospreys woo to their mate;

That coos on the river ait.

Fair and gracious maiden;

Well matched for courting gentlemen.

Water cress of varying height;

Adrift on both left and right;

Fair and gracious lass;

Pursue day and night, no less.

In vain they court;

For days and night they hold the ladies in their thought.

Their hearts are saddened with ache,

And they toss around in bed.

Water cress of varying height;

Pick and choose from either left or right.

Fair and gracious lady;

Tune their harp and lutes in melody.

Water cress of varying height;

Selecting from either left or right.

air and gracious lady;

Nuptial bells (and drum) ring with gaiety.

關關雎鳩、在河之洲。　窈窕淑女、君子好逑。

參差荇菜、左右流之。　窈窕淑女、寤寐求之。

求之不得、寤寐思服。　悠哉悠哉、輾轉反側。

參差荇菜、左右采之。　窈窕淑女、琴瑟友之。

參差荇菜、左右芼之。　窈窕淑女、鍾鼓樂之。

Note:

This is a very popular poem in the Classic, Book of Song.

Stopping By Woods On A Snowy Evening by Robert Frost: An Appreciation

The main theme is about choices and balances in everyday life for a mundane traveller, and about conflict between the beauty of nature and the reality of human civilisation, family-social responsibility and personal freedom, rationality and emotionality. Often the two polarities are difficult to co-exist simultaneously, and each has to choose his/her own path.

The narrator writes as a first person in the present tense, or present continuous, and it is, therefore, easy to identify oneself with the lone traveller along the same journey. The simple diction and smooth flow of syntax renders the theme in lively and evocative way. He is "stopping by" (or "stopping here") to appreciate the awe and beauty of the "whose woods" in a cold "snowy evening". The alliteration with the assonance of "O" sound is music to begin with. It's winter and there's no birds cooing; perhaps it's the narrator's heart murmuring from the start, motivating him to respond. The narrator is aware of trespassing, but the owner, he reckons, is in the "village though"; the last word betrays his uncertainty, or rather he thinks no one can claim ownership of beauty or truth, if "woods" stands for that "lovely, dark and deep" symbol of wilderness. Though he/she has "miles and miles to go", he prefers the momentary joy of escaping from reality. The woods "fill with snow"; a hyperbole to show it is deep winter (solstice). It's very cold for the lakes are frozen, and a landscape of white in a dark evening. The auditory sound from harness bell and the music of "sweep of easy wind" (onomatopoeia), with the youthful and pure flake (downy flake) enchanted the landscape. He enjoys his solitude. The personification of the horse, asking whether he is of right mind to be there, implies he really has a companion. Perhaps he's other self is doing the asking. However, he has to surrender his choice, for he has "promises" (symbol for family or social obligations) to keep, "before I sleep", another symbol for death, silence or dream, depending on the narrator. "Miles and miles" are more metaphorical than literal. The skillful use of figurative language has effectively conveyed the theme, in whatever the narrator interprets.

What captivates me the most in "The woods" is the endless reflection and discovery on multiple reading, and that the feeling changes with personal mood and circumstances.

First, the narrator transcends the mundane of everyday life into some uncertain wonder or beauty. There's the natural setting of rural life, compared with my busy, city life. Reading the text lifts up the spirit, and, thereby, propels into a different realm or reality, into some unexpected excitement—the movement of emotion to unite with the intellect. Echoing "The woods", I feel there's really something that's indeed "lovely, dark and deep."

Secondly, the readers are presented with thesis and anti-thesis, rationality and emotionality, the Road and its alternative paths, paradoxes and pathos, the here and there, for reflection and interpretation. This is achieved beautifully using symbols, images, metaphor and other figurative language, and turning them into allegories.

Third, I like its brevity. "The woods" contains only four sets of quadrant, that is, a mere sixteen lines—easy to recite with pleasure and a joy to memorise. It can be frustrating to decipher a difficult text.

Lastly, "The woods" has inspired me to compose these lines to continue with the course, despite its hectic assignment.

> Before I go to sleep, go to sleep;
> Stop by Open U to take a peep.
> Doing and mapping English Literature: ache or cake?
> Weaving small and big letters, my cold hands shake.
> Winter is now over, the landscape clearer;
> Without the harness horse, I ride freer.
> Fear of dementia and everlasting slumber;
> Before the grave, I crave to remember.

References:

1. Stephen Matterson & Darryl Jones (2000), Studying Poetry, Arnold, UK.
2. Spark Notes (2008), How To Write Poetry, Spark Publishing, USA.

FLICKERING FLAME (Chinese)

闪烁的火焰

舞躍在五顏六色, 那光芒中.

搖曳火焰, 此刻忽隱忽現, 火兒累了.

反映生命的鏡子, 老化的裸體,

懊悔和恐懼,

時候脫下工作的外衣,

無掩飾, 自由飄拂.

在前餘燼太弱難點燃,

那的火焰, 那的柔和微風,

呼喚著, 重新重新開始,

喚醒那火焰和心靈,

砰的一聲, 打破了沉默,

那光芒重活起來,

這是生命的詩歌.

FIREFLY (Chinese)

螢火蟲

在陰影下,
孤独發光的螢火蟲,
傳發編碼的光,
慰撫一個人和其困境.
牠是小的
光亮不高.
在黑暗中
牠的閃光是明亮,
發光;
在神聖的配合.
一粒微塵的火花;
顯出黑暗的視覺.

TRAPPED EGO (Chinese)

自我被困

在一個飄忽的歲月;
拉拉推推到邊緣.
無情歲月推迫人老;
紋身疼痛是錯誤.
被困是自我發光的失敗;
搖荡在半露和陰影之間.
害怕涉足光明;
陰影將離開視線.

WHO ARE WE? (Chinese)

我們是誰?

瞭望世界是用眼睛, 眼光有相對的意見;

聆聽是用耳朵, 但不用心聆聽旁人的哭泣.

嗅覺用鼻子, 思索比氣味感到更多;

真相和半真理往往是弄不明.

精美的菜餚喜嘗其滋味;

吃得匆忙結果是浪費.

我們希望找到什麼, 尋求什麼;

神聖宗教是壯嚴.

如果缺乏藝術要問智慧

你的意向分散不集中.

我們敲打每戶的扇門;

找不到那傾心的.

我們是誰? 再問一次;

誰是我們真正的智能.

BUCKET LIST (Chinese)

臨終遺願

他們堅持要查看我的遺願清單;

懸垂棺里是缺失的要點.

活得尊貴, 死無尊嚴;

他們所有的折磨最終消失了.

家庭優先, 但沒有備件和護理;

關係損傷, 不喜分享.

在世時, 你是管理;

在快要死了, 功耗天坑.

未實現的夢想和願望;

不和諧很難重修好.

當活著時没有緊急的辦理;

健康財富和邏輯都是虛構的.

年青和壯健的一輩或許無法呼吸魅力;

夢想和希望,出售予迫害者.

如果任何人強調要看我的黑名單;

爬進我棺材里與我幽會.

RIDDLE OF CHINESE
PICTOGRAPHS (Chinese)

中文象形圖之謎

要理解中國人的智力,

搜索五千年的歷史發现.

生活中的簾幕, 顯示該標誌

畫像和圖片, 象形文字.

文明的開始, 諸多復雜.

字詞與自由基, 在體操,

舞蹈有它自己的調性音樂,　盛行同步

進入藝術和書法,

符號和語義

探戈舞或在三重奏組曲.

象形演變成意音文字

和表意符號

一種古代語言的誕生,

一個自豪文明的民族.

這是陰陽文化,

社會和諧無壓力和苦痛, 文反映眾多因素.

吃, 這個字詞

來自一雙自由基,

含意討求一口.

反映一個持續貧窮的歷史,

朝代的改變, 造成內戰,

外國侵掠, 強姦;

中國經過苛刻獲得經驗.

保持國民的需要,

領導人供應糧食滿足國民的需求.

糧食的重要性,

宴請和烹調文化在家中,

其次, 親屬們.

對命運的表意文字描述

人的第一優先是

屈服于什麼樣的命運, 或聽從

上級的命令, 宿命論

不是中國哲學, 當貧困的時代,

改變上升叛乱, 不是服從; 在暴動,

風險帶來的機會, 要變換命運,

開放自由的大門.

尚未人類有局限性.

我們無能改變形勢,

命運最終接受.

當所有的努力都失敗,

語言和文化互相滋養

和團結是分不開的.　在古代的象形圖,

觀察到中國人的智慧.

MUSING IN THE MORNING (Chinese)

沉思在早上

排隊在新加坡飲食攤販;
我的關節裂聲緩慢爬行.
在這裡的粥菜是最好的;
多汁的肉丸垂涎下胸膛.
一杯咖啡隆起早上精神.
整天精力持續良好常態.
通過翻閱首頁的新聞錄;
查看強奸抢劫种族虐待.
無法尋找值得閱讀頁面;
傷眼癈物新聞讓人不安.
眼中淚水充滿靜暗自流;
毛氈子包著並將它棄掉.

INTIMATE SEXUALITY (Chinese)

親蜜的欲望

在半夜里,
靈魂被熱騰喚醒,
抓住此刻,
柔弱帶來熱情,
充滿情感, 熱情的刺激
沉重的呼吸.
床褥弄亂與枕邊伴.
開放擁抱和逗弄,
她的心靈嵌入藝術的漲潮,
和贈予鮮艳沐浴的分泌液,
進入極大的欢乐.
他們喃喃的親吻.

OVERCAST SKY (Chinese)

陰暗的天空

永遠擦不掉一個墨漬的記憶；
選舉的更換本可洗去愚蠢。
指著手指給予他們投票；
僅有鈔票能把船傾覆。
飛行外人搶了風頭　；
海嘯無法推翻。
遊戲從不公平，部隊不遺餘力；
政權勢力巨吹奏，无畏于絕望。
沒有鑼鼓鳴或敲鈸聲；
污腐敗，無色彩，是鬥爭的號笛。

DIFFERENT WORLD (Chinese)

不同的世界

碧空光亮的魅力;
來自遙遠隧道發出的光.
母親, 最佳神態, 站立在那裡;
遇見傳奇風情的朋友.
平靜和光亮, 漂浮在空中;
撕掉青年流淚敖夜在身上;
在大堂微風吹拂她們的青絲.
活力充沛不容長期逗留;
微風吹起飛飄到另一個世界.

SHARING (Chinese)

分 享

不要握住我的手
不要咬
只是溫柔的舔舔

嘴唇的感動
滋味甜蜜柔軟
難以抗拒
取一個
融化在嘴裡
快樂在心中

她給我推開
遵守諾言

但怎樣
勸說
一個可愛不願意的孩子

分享
她最喜歡的巧克力雪糕錐

品味和滴淋淋
滴在她的冰涼小手上
她享受地，舔著和流涎著
爺爺

SISTERLY LOVE (Chinese)

姊 妹 情

窗外微風吹來嗡嗡聲；

椰子枝葉跟她們的影子玩精靈.

行雷閃電砸向她們的力氣.

禱告神們正確的目標.

我的寶兒們如何度過那焦躁的兩周；

坐困在家沒有滑板的激動.

困擾為何惡巫侵染她的嘴；

水泡和成坑狀的疼痛并呻喊.

把自己鎖住在房間, 嬰孩妹妹好；

一個六歲可愛的她真如銀鐘噹噹響.

蹣跚學步從陽臺窗外傳音信.

願望她的姊姊復康并出一起踏滑板.

LAVENDER, MY LOVE (Chinese)

熏衣草，我的喜愛

她離開

她的靜落裡，

腳尖站著，

低著頭，

生氣在沉默，

自己喃喃細語，

悶著氣，一會兒.

她哭喊起來，

對孩子的愛，

唯一的關懷.

摟我，

擁抱我，

抱起我，

只是我先，

她怕羞的回避，

不再欣賞

學校，溜走了時間

離家,
剝奪孩子,
愛好的玩耍.
甜蜜,可靠的哄慰,
為愛要
不是羞怯的共享,
與新生的
嬰兒弟弟.

HURT MEMORIES (Chinese)

傷害的回憶

混沌痛苦的回憶
穿過
她的思維，她的心扉
如同一卷不斷的電視劇。
在選擇性，引人的重演，
她緊握住損傷，
不必要的憂痛，
如一塊青紫痕，無聊貓
戲弄受驚老鼠。
強迫的行為
記憶
傷害感情，背离
愛與恨是
如此令人費解，
所以經久
胸膛疼痛

嘮叨不停，

如臃腫的空氣

含漱液在腸子里。

無能忘記

過去傷痕，

繼續註冊

那同樣的責備，

並指責遊戲，

次復次的，

像融冰解凍，

重次凍結，并每個冷顫的。

覆蓋愛情

在過去，現在或

將來，這是什麼的自由

記住、忘記，

什麼必要

被遺忘，或已被遺忘的。

運行或下臺

在一個厭倦的踏車上

心悸及脉沖，

進行联系或共鳴

在線路曲折迂迴

不容易克制

聰明技巧轉向刺痛。

一個簡單的道歉，

一個真誠的懺悔，

一個逾步的倒退，

沒有多餘的話語

或思考。是如此容易

尚未非常，非常困難

使那移動

释放

的傷害，而

要堅持

恢復活力

論愛情，永遠

如此的苦甜。

NIAGARA FALLS (Chinese)

尼亞加拉大瀑布

在馬蹄,

浩如煙海妖嬈, 瓢潑大雨.

來自各地的崇拜者, 聚集有愛

洶湧的激流, 雷鳴般的洪流中

擊起她的鼓.烟熏的霧激起了她的魅力.

濺起閃亮的水花.

她的光澤, 她的原始之美,

整個大洲的驕傲.

敢於崩潰,

她的根底於船.

或走在瀑布的边缘,

風險走近, 僅為感受的快感,

生活. 暖和的誘惑,

那冰凍的世俗,

野外有力量,

在那冷凍常式帶來一股熱血.

HEAVENLY TOUR OF WUYISHAN (Chinese)

武夷山的天堂之遊

洪亮聲音穿過裂隙和洞穴, 聽不到老虎的吼叫;
我们爬, 没有任何登山武藝踏上天遊峰.
窥视缝隙的光圈并無神女浴.
菩萨在高峰禁止我们向上路径.
在山座下, 罗漢茶和岩石木耳是當地促進產品;
皇帝紅袍的六個灌木叢在懸崖上是割喉的高價格.
從上游下的六座竹筏行;
雄麗三峽, 蜿蜒曲折, 漫遊在白日夢中.
書法與朦朧岩石形成的極樂,
崖璧吊棺喚醒塵世間的靈魂什麼是差錯.

THIS IS MY STORY OF SINGAPORE (Chinese)

這是我的新加坡故事

死于新加坡的沙灘
馬奎斯遺留他的羊皮紙，
煉金術，在沼澤的深淵，
對智慧和勤勉
的發現，魔術和才智，
重生的另一個
城國，那古代的王子，
由一個權力公司的職員，
他看到那小貓
變為獅子，這麼稱它，
魔幻術語，
那良師的眼淚，
黃金花瓣與黃金鱼，
成為一條魚尾獅，接受
辛勤苦力及廢選者，
從中國沿海，那智力

從北部和附近的居地，

無歧視的顏色，

由貧瘠的轉進為一個

現代的大都市，一個小小

步不穩的島嶼，稱聯合

組別，持久

幾乎半個世紀。

它將持續下去，祇要

意識到的系統

語言文化與腐化。

各異小型的群體，

能在內部調整和諧，

外部重進一個

不停變化的世界。